EARTH AND
THE INNER
PLANETS

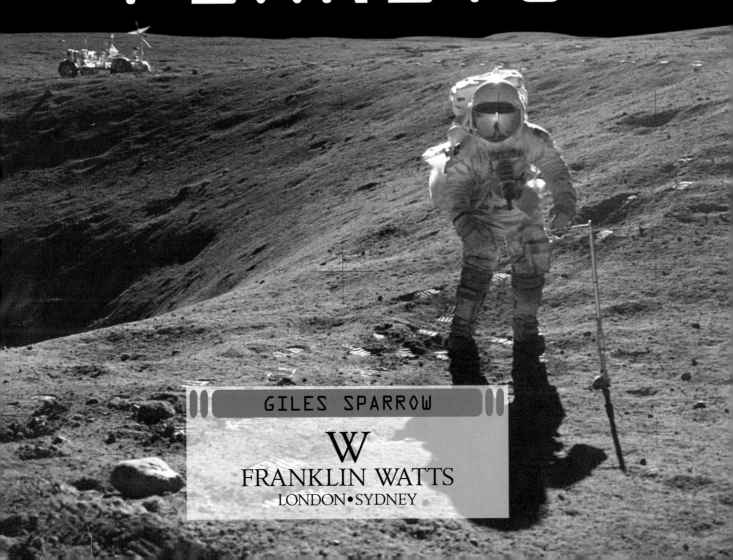

GILES SPARROW

W
FRANKLIN WATTS
LONDON • SYDNEY

First published in 2011 by
Franklin Watts
338 Euston Road
London NW1 3BH

Franklin Watts Australia
Level 17/207 Kent Street
Sydney NSW 2000

Conceived and produced by Tall Tree Ltd
Cartoons: Guy Harvey

A CIP catalogue record for this book is available
from the British Library.

Dewey Classification: 919.9'204

ISBN: 978 0 7496 9577 4

Printed in China

Franklin Watts is a division of Hachette Children's
Books, an Hachette UK company.

www.hachette.co.uk

Picture credits:
t-top, b-bottom, l-left, r-right, c-centre
All images courtesy of NASA, except:
12b Dreamstime.com/Xavier Marchant,
14b US Geological Survey,
15t Dreamstime.com/Luke Pederson,
16bl Dreamstime.com/Ian Scott,
17cr Dreamstime.com/Robert Hardholt,
18-19b Dreamstime.com/Stasys Eidiejus,
19tl istockphoto.com/Lucky-Photos,
29b Dreamstime.com/Paul Van Eykelen

Disclaimer
The website addresses (URLs) included in this book
were valid at the time of going to press. However,
because of the nature of the Internet, it is possible
that some addresses have changed, or sites may
have changed or closed down since publication.
While the author and publisher regret any
inconvenience this may cause to readers, no
responsibility for any such changes can be
accepted by either the author or the publisher.

This book describes a fictional journey into outer
space. It is not possible for humans to travel to
the inner planets with present-day technology.
Readers are invited to use their imaginations to
journey around our solar system.

Words in **bold** are in the glossary on page 30.

Contents

The local neighbourhood

Get ready to blast off on the trip of a lifetime! We're off on a mission to explore the **worlds** of the inner **solar system** – Mercury, Venus and Mars – as well as our own **planet** Earth and its Moon. The solar system consists of our nearest star (the Sun) and everything that circles around it.

BALL OF FIRE

The Sun (right) is a huge ball of exploding gas, much larger than any planet. Like all heavy objects it produces a pull called **gravity**. This stops fast-moving objects flying off into space and instead traps them in circular or oval paths called **orbits**.

THE SOLAR SYSTEM

The objects that orbit the Sun fall into two regions – the inner and outer solar systems. The inner solar system is a warm area close to the Sun, and contains four small planets that are mostly made of rock – Mercury, Venus, Earth and Mars. There are various other smaller worlds – Earth's Moon and the tiny **satellites** (moons) of Mars, plus the asteroids, most of which lie in a belt beyond Mars. The outer solar system, in contrast, is cold and dominated by gas and ice rather than rock. It contains four giant planets – Jupiter, Saturn, Uranus and Neptune. They are spread over a much wider area and surrounded by a variety of smaller moons and **comets**.

Our tour of the solar system will start with Mercury, the planet closest to the Sun. From there, we will travel away from the Sun, visiting Venus, Earth and the Moon, before moving on to Mars and the asteroid belt. Each of the **astronomical bodies** we'll visit is a world in its own right, with its own days, seasons and years, its own unique features – and its own hazards. It's going to be a fun trip, but it could also be a dangerous one!

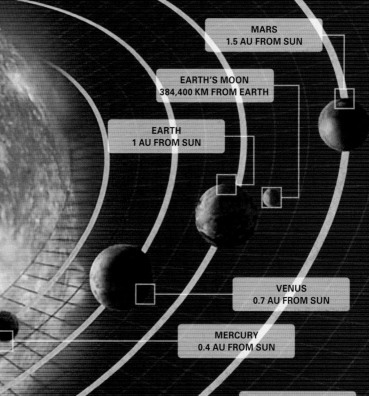

MARS
1.5 AU FROM SUN

EARTH'S MOON
384,400 KM FROM EARTH

EARTH
1 AU FROM SUN

VENUS
0.7 AU FROM SUN

MERCURY
0.4 AU FROM SUN

ASTEROID BELT
2.8 AU FROM SUN

NEED TO KNOW

You'll need strong sun block for your trip to Mercury and Venus, and warm clothes for visiting chilly Mars! Earth is 150 million kilometres from the Sun – this is one astronomical unit, or AU. Mercury and Venus are closer to the Sun than the Earth, but Mars is further away. When measured in astronomical units, the distances from the Sun are as follows: Mercury = 0.4 AU; Venus = 0.7 AU; Mars = 1.5 AU; asteroid belt = 2.8 AU.

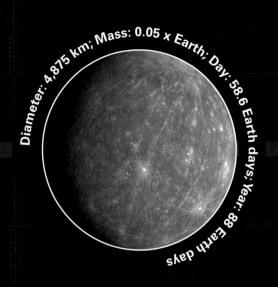

Diameter: 4,875 km; Mass: 0.05 x Earth; Day: 58.6 Earth days; Year: 88 Earth days

Mercury

Mercury is a special world in many ways – it's the smallest of the planets and the fastest moving. It's also the closest to the Sun and suffers the biggest variations in temperature. As a result, Mercury is a parched, airless ball of cratered rock. Despite the daytime heat, it's not the best holiday destination!

SPEEDY PLANET

Mercury races round the Sun at about 50 kilometres per second, so you'll need a fast spacecraft to keep up with it. Although it orbits the Sun in just 88 days, it takes a surprisingly long 59 days to spin on its axis. As a result, most parts of the planet have a day and a night that both last for an entire Mercury year. During the baking days, temperatures on the side facing the Sun can reach 430°C, while at night it plunges to a frozen -170°C.

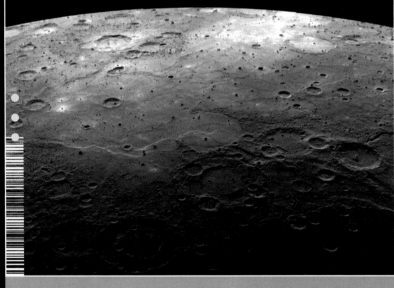

Mercury is similar in appearance to Earth's Moon. It is heavily cratered with regions of smooth plains, and has no natural satellites. Unlike the Moon, it has a large iron core, which generates a weak magnetic field, about 1 per cent as strong as that of the Earth.

At 1,340 kilometres across, Mercury's Caloris Basin is one of the biggest **impact craters** in the solar system. But although it's wide, it's not very deep – the asteroid collision that created it was so powerful that it cracked the planet's crust and allowed molten rock to erupt upwards and fill in the centre. Today, the most impressive features are the surrounding rings of mountains and the ray-like ridges, which formed where rocks from the impact were blasted out across the nearby surface.

NOT TO MISS

WEIRD TERRAIN: *An area where shockwaves from the Caloris smash met up on the other side of Mercury and shook the landscape to pieces.*

DISCOVERY RUPES: *A huge cliff, 650 kilometres long and 2 kilometres high, this is one of many such cliffs on Mercury, which are known as rupes. They seem to mark places where the planet's crust has been pulled apart and jammed back together.*

THE SPIDER: *Dozens of mysterious cracks stretch out like a spider's legs around this crater (see below).*

POLAR ICE: *Astronomers believe that craters at Mercury's poles may contain deep-frozen ice dumped by comet crashes.*

The surface of the Caloris Basin is covered with lava flows and rocky ridges.

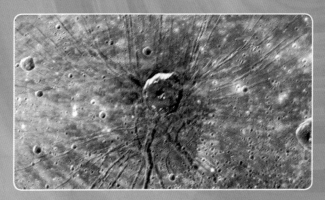

Diameter: 12,104 km; Mass: 0.82 x Earth; Day: 243 Earth days; Year: 224.7 Earth days

Venus

It may be named after the Roman goddess of beauty and look like a brilliant white jewel from space but, in reality, Venus is a fearsome place. Try to land there and you'll find yourself being crushed by the atmospheric pressure, choked by toxic gases and burnt to death by poisonous vapour – all at the same time!

BRILLIANT CLOUDS

Venus's thick clouds hide its surface from sight, and appear to blaze with reflected sunlight. Even from up close, the planet looks featureless, and you have to filter the light (the equivalent of wearing sunglasses) to see the huge arrow patterns in the atmosphere. High winds carry these patterns around the planet once every four days, but Venus's own rotation is far slower – in fact its rotation period, or day, (which lasts for 243 Earth days) is longer than its year (224.7 Earth days)!

MAXWELL'S MOUNTAINS: *This region of volcanic peaks includes Mount Gula (4 kilometres high and 275 kilometres across) and Mount Sif (2 kilometres high and 300 kilometres wide).*

ALPHA REGIO: *A raised region of the surface, scattered with strange flattened 'pancake domes', formed where lava oozed out of the surface.*

LAVINIA REGIO CRATERS: *A group of three craters, each 40–50 kilometres across, which formed when a chunk of rock from space broke into fragments and slammed into the surface.*

VENUSIAN VALLEYS: *These huge, winding canyons running near Venus's equator may show where the crust once tried to break into* **plates.**

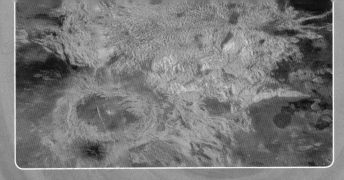

This three-dimensional view of Venus's surface shows part of the Alpha Regio, which is raised above the surrounding terrain to a height of 1–2 kilometres. The light-coloured rock is thought to be older than the darker, surrounding volcanic plains.

DEADLY ATMOSPHERE

The thick layer of gases that makes up Venus's atmosphere is very dense – it exerts 100 times the pressure of Earth's atmosphere. Dominated by carbon dioxide gas, Venus's atmosphere produces a powerful greenhouse effect, trapping nearly all of the heat from the Sun and heating the surface of the planet to about 470°C. If that weren't bad enough, there are sulphurous clouds in the atmosphere, which means that it often rains corrosive sulphuric acid.

The surface of Venus is a barren, desolate place. Images from **Venera 13** *show flat chunks of volcanic rock littered around a dark soil surface.*

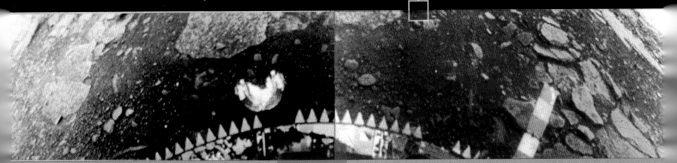

These pictures of the surface of Venus were taken by the Russian **Venera 13** *space probe. Its descent vehicle, or lander, touched down on 1 March 1982, landing in a raised area callled the Phoebe Regio. When put together, these two separate photographs from the lander's cameras show the surface around the landing site. Despite being equipped with heavy protective shielding, the lander stopped sending data after two hours and seven minutes.*

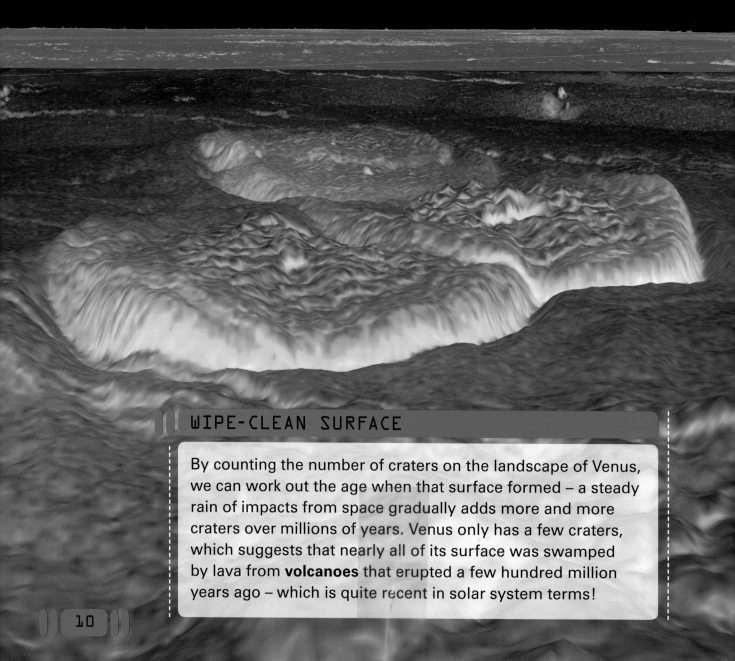

Radar views of Venus's surface, such as the one below, show that volcanic activity shaped its appearance. Molten rock erupted from inside the planet before solidifying to form towering peaks, flattened domes and vast plains of lava. We can't be sure if Venus's volcanoes are still active – see if you can find out!

WIPE-CLEAN SURFACE

By counting the number of craters on the landscape of Venus, we can work out the age when that surface formed – a steady rain of impacts from space gradually adds more and more craters over millions of years. Venus only has a few craters, which suggests that nearly all of its surface was swamped by lava from **volcanoes** that erupted a few hundred million years ago – which is quite recent in solar system terms!

If you're planning to explore on the surface of Venus, you'll need a heavyweight armoured suit that can resist high temperatures – the surface is hot enough to fry an egg on it! The suit will need to be tough enough to withstand the crushing atmospheric pressure and corrosion from acid rain. Hydraulic joints will also be required to help you cope with the suit's weight. Venus isn't a place to hang around. The first Russian Venera spaceprobes, sent into the atmosphere in the 1960s, were destroyed before they reached the ground. Even the heavily shielded probes that landed from the 1970s onwards broke down and lost contact with Earth!

HIDDEN SURFACE

Venus's choking atmosphere keeps the planet's surface hidden from view. The only way to 'see' the surface is using radar, bouncing radio signals from space off the landscape and measuring the way they are reflected back. This data is converted into visual images. By firing enough radar beams, you can build up a map of the whole planet. Venus is only a little smaller than Earth, but it doesn't have quite the right conditions for the surface to crack into plates – instead the outer crust seems to be one single piece.

Radar mapping of Venus's surface has enabled scientists to create pictures of the terrain, revealing that the planet has many large mountain ranges.

11

Earth

Diameter: ... kg; Day: 23 hours 56 minutes; Year: 365.25 days

Earth is the largest world in the inner solar system, and is unique thanks to its geology, its abundant water and its life. From space it looks like a 'blue marble', dominated by water and surrounded by a thin but vital atmosphere of nitrogen, oxygen and clouds of water vapour.

WATERWORLD

Roughly two-thirds of Earth's surface is covered in water, forming large oceans. Here, the water gets mixed with dissolved minerals from rocks and chemicals from decayed animal life, both of which turn it salty. On average, the oceans are 3,800 metres deep, but there are some deep ocean trenches that go down to 10,900 metres. Water on Earth is constantly shifting between vapour, liquid and frozen forms, in a water cycle that helps to drive Earth's weather systems, control its climate and erode (wear down) its surface.

AIR AND CLIMATE

Earth's atmosphere is 78 per cent nitrogen and 21 per cent oxygen. There are small amounts of other gases, including a vital 0.04 per cent carbon dioxide, which traps heat near Earth's surface and helps to keep the planet warm. Shifting air currents carry heat away from the warm equator (which receives more sunlight) and towards the much colder poles. Earth's daily rotation also helps to drive winds in certain directions, and the condensation and evaporation of water vapour helps to create Earth's huge variety of weather patterns, from droughts to ferocious thunderstorms.

Gases in Earth's atmosphere help to protect us from lethal space radiation.

Earth's atmosphere blankets our planet with a layer of gases that become thinner and thinner with increasing altitude. The boundary between the atmosphere and outer space is about 100 kilometres from Earth's surface.

TRAVELLER'S TIPS - THE GOLDILOCKS ZONE

Earth owes its abundant water to its position in the solar system – orbiting at a distance of 150 million kilometres, it's neither too hot nor too cold, but just right – like Goldilocks's porridge! About 4.6 billion years ago, when the planets were forming, there was plenty of water spread across the solar system. All the water on Venus boiled away into space, and most (if not all) of that on Mars froze solid. The only other places in the solar system that have large amounts of liquid water are moons in the outer solar system. Even there, any water must be trapped beneath a solid crust so that it doesn't boil away into space.

Earth's surface

Earth's surface may look calm from space, but it's in a state of constant change. Forces deep inside the planet split the outer crust into a series of plates and push them around like jigsaw pieces. Volcanic eruptions and earthquakes are constantly reshaping the surface.

Earth's solid crust floats on a deep layer of semi-molten rock called the mantle. Flowing currents in this mantle push the plates of crust around. Underneath the oceans, the plates are thin – the oceanic crust is 5–10 kilometres thick. Major landmasses are made from much thicker continental crust, 30–50 kilometres thick and with deep 'roots' below the surface. Where plates are pulling apart (usually underwater), volcanic eruptions from the mantle create new crust. Where plates collide, one plate may be pushed under the other, creating a chain of volcanoes; or one may be pushed over the other to create a huge mountain range.

In 1980, the eruption of Mount St Helens – an active volcano forming part of a mountain range in Washington, USA – blasted a huge plume of ash and rock into the air.

Aurorae light up the night sky with a shimmering greenish or faint red glow. They occur most often from September to October and from March to April.

MOLTEN CORE

At the centre of the Earth lies an enormous ball of molten and solid metal – the core. Mostly made from iron and nickel, this spinning ball is about a quarter of the planet's entire diameter. As it spins, the core produces a powerful magnetic field that emerges near Earth's poles. This field extends out into space, where it sweeps up harmful particles from the Sun and diverts them harmlessly to rain down in Earth's poles creating spectacular 'aurorae' – the northern and southern lights.

NOT TO MISS

THE PACIFIC OCEAN: *Earth's largest ocean, the Pacific, contains more than 45 per cent of the entire planet's surface water.*

THE HIMALAYAS: *The highest mountain range on Earth, towering more than 8,000 metres above sea level and forced upwards by the collision between the Indian and Asian continental plates.*

THE ANDES: *A 7,000-kilometre-long mountain range formed as the Pacific Ocean's Nazca Plate is forced beneath the South American continental plate.*

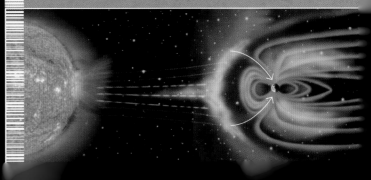

The Sun emits a stream of particles, called the solar wind, that shoots out into space. These particles are drawn towards Earth's poles by its electromagnetic field.

The living planet

Earth is the only place in the solar system that we know supports life. Millions of different species – ranging from towering trees and enormous whales to countless insects and tiny bacteria – survive and thrive across the surface of our beautiful blue-green planet.

VARIETY OF LIFE

Life on Earth takes a huge range of forms, from single-celled bacteria to fungi, plants and animals made from millions of individual cells. Plants and animals make up nearly all of the larger life on the planet. Plants are mostly fixed in place, and turn sunlight and carbon dioxide from the atmosphere into food and energy. Animals usually move around, gathering energy by eating plants or other animals.

This photograph shows Earth from space at night. The white dots are man-made lights, found in highly developed or populated areas of Earth's surface.

The Great Barrier Reef off the northeast coast of Australia supports a huge variety of sea life, including many species of fish, sea turtles, dolphins and whales.

More than 6 billion people can be found scattered across Earth's surface. Humans are intelligent animals with the ability to alter the environment, building cities to live in, and farming plants and animals for food. But our huge numbers and advanced technology have given us the power to change our planet beyond recognition. These changes have led to the extinction of many species of animal, damage to the natural environment and the threat of global climate change.

NOT TO MISS

THE GREAT MIGRATIONS: *Every year millions of wildebeest, zebra and other grazing animals travel back and forth across the East African grasslands in a seasonal search for fresh food (see below).*

THE KUMBH MELA: *Every 12 years, tens of millions of Hindu pilgrims converge on the joining point of the Ganges, Yamuna and Saraswati rivers at Allahabad in northern India.*

THE BLUE WHALE: *The largest animal on the planet, this enormous seagoing mammal reaches lengths of up to 33 metres, but feeds on tiny shrimp-like animals called krill.*

THE BURJ KHALIFA: *The tallest building in the world, this spire-like skyscraper soars to a height of 818 metres and has 160 floors.*

The Moon

The Moon is Earth's constant companion in space, and the largest satellite compared to its planet in all the solar system.
It was created 4.5 billion years ago, when a Mars-sized planet smashed into the young Earth, throwing debris into space that clumped together to create the Moon.

PHASES OF THE MOON

The Moon spins on its axis in exactly the same time it takes to go round the Earth (a lunar month). This means that the inhabitants of Earth can only ever see one side of the Moon, with the other permanently hidden from view. The amount of sunlight shining onto the Earth-facing nearside changes through each month, creating the Moon's distinctive phases.

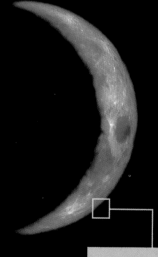

The Waxing Crescent phase of the Moon, as it moves out of shadow.

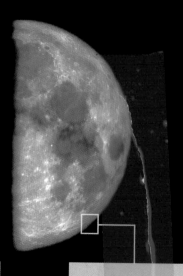

The First Quarter phase of the Moon.

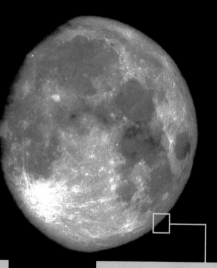

The Waxing Gibbous phase of the Moon.

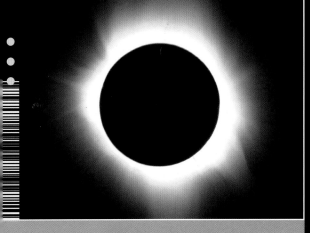

A solar eclipse takes place when the Moon – passing between the Sun and Earth – fully or partially covers the Sun and blocks out, or eclipses, the star's light.

ECLIPSES

By a strange coincidence, the Moon is 400 times smaller than the Sun, but also 400 times closer to Earth. This means that the Moon and Sun appear almost exactly the same size when viewed from the Earth. The Moon's orbit around Earth is slightly tilted, so the three objects rarely line up with each other. When they do line up, the result is a stunning solar eclipse (see above).

SEA OF TRANQUILITY: *A vast lunar lava plain and site of the Apollo 11 mission in 1969, when the first humans set foot on the Moon (see below).*

TYCHO: *One of the youngest and best preserved of the many impact craters on the lunar surface, the 85 kilometre-wide Tycho is about 100 million years old. It is surrounded by bright rays stretching across 1,500 kilometres of the lunar landscape.*

HADLEY RILLE: *More than 85 kilometres long, this narrow winding valley through the lunar surface is the collapsed remains of an underground lava tunnel.*

THE LUNAR APENNINES: *This 225-kilometre-long mountain range marks the rim of a huge crater in which an ancient lava plain, the Sea of Showers, was formed.*

The Full Moon phase occurs when the Moon is completely lit up (see below left). A Waning Crescent phase (see below, right) is one phase away from a New Moon phase, when the Moon's nearside is entirely dark.

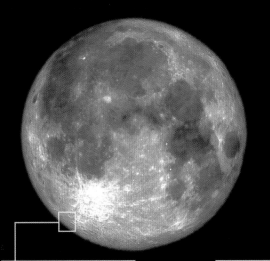

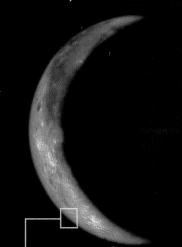

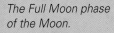

The Full Moon phase of the Moon.

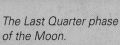

The Last Quarter phase of the Moon.

The Waning Crescent phase of the Moon, as it moves into shadow.

Cratered surface

The Moon is too small to hold onto a protective atmosphere, so every speck of cosmic dust hits it like a tiny bullet, helping to smash up the surface. The result is that the Moon is covered in craters and powdery soil – this can make getting about a little tricky!

CRATERS UPON CRATERS

Given time, the surface activity on larger planets (such as volcanoes, wind and rain) can wipe away traces of even the largest craters. But for most of the Moon's history, its surface has only been shaped by impact craters, so any footprints you leave on the Moon will be undisturbed for millions of years. Old craters are often overlaid with younger ones, while the most recent are still surrounded by bright rays made from pulverised rock that was thrown out by the collisions.

*Located on the Moon's far side, the 75-kilometre-wide King Crater was photographed by the **Apollo 16** mission in 1972. Smaller impact craters can be seen inside the main crater.*

HIGHLANDS AND SEAS

Even from a distance, you'll notice that the lunar surface comes in two distinct varieties – bright, hilly and heavily cratered highlands, and dark, flat regions with fewer craters. The highlands are the remains of the Moon's original surface, covered in 4 billion years' worth of craters. The flat areas are called 'seas'. They are ancient lava plains that formed when volcanic rock erupted to fill in low-lying 'basins'.

On the Apollo 17 moon mission, American astronaut Harrison Schmitt collected rocks from the lunar highlands to take back to Earth for scientists to study.

This panoramic photograph shows the hilly, rock-strewn surface of the Camelot Crater in the Taurus-Littrow region of the Moon, near the Apollo 17 landing site. The picture, with the tiny figure of astronaut Harrison Schmitt in the background, was taken by the Apollo 17 crew commander, astronaut Eugene Cernan.

TRAVELLER'S TIPS – HOW TO BUILD A MOONBASE

Surviving on the Moon's surface for a long period of time takes a lot of work. First you'll want to build a heavily shielded base to protect you from dangerous cosmic rays and the heat of the Sun. The Moon's low gravity (just one-sixth of Earth's) should help you with this construction project. Second, you'll need water. You could try digging for ice in some of the permanently shadowed craters around the north and south poles – just like similar craters on Mercury, these may hide deep-frozen comet ice. You'll also need power – solar panels are fine for half of each month, but during the long lunar night (equal to 14 Earth days) you'll need a backup!

Mars

The outermost of the rocky planets, Mars is smaller than both Earth and Venus, and considerably colder. But with its thin atmosphere, icy polar caps and pattern of days and seasons, the Red Planet is the most Earth-like of the solar system's other worlds, and the one most likely to harbour life.

WELCOME TO THE RED PLANET

Mars gets its name from its distinctive red colour, which inspired ancient astronomers to think of the Roman god of war. However, once you get up close, the truth behind Mars's colour is revealed – Martian rock and sand contain large amounts of iron oxide, the chemical that forms rust. The atmosphere, meanwhile, is mostly poisonous carbon dioxide, and is so thin that it can't protect Mars from huge temperature changes. The Martian surface varies between -90°C and 0°C (freezing point) in a typical day – a little chilly, so pack your thermal underwear.

*This amazing photograph, taken by the **Mars Exploration Rover** in 2006, shows the reddish, rocky terrain of the Erebus Crater, an old, eroded crater about 350 metres wide.*

DOGS OF WAR

Mars has two small moons called Phobos (top right) and Deimos (below right). Each is an uneven lump of rock just a few kilometres across. They are almost certainly stray asteroids that escaped from the main asteroid belt, which were caught up in Mars's gravity when they came too close to the Red Planet. Orbiting in just 7 hours 40 minutes, Phobos is doomed to destruction – it is slowly spiralling closer to Mars, and will eventually hit it. Make sure you come back in 11 million years to see that!

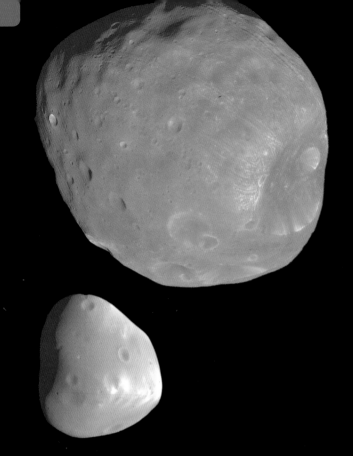

LIFE ON MARS

Astronomers on Earth have always been fascinated by the idea of life on Mars. In the 1870s, an Italian stargazer called Schiaparelli claimed he could see long straight channels connecting up the darker parts of the Martian surface. Soon, other astronomers also reported seeing them, and suggested that they might be a canal system built by intelligent Martians to carry water from the polar icecaps to other parts of the planet. Photographs eventually proved that the canals were an illusion. More recently, NASA scientists claimed to have found a less impressive sign of life – fossilised microbes (microscopic creatures) in a piece of Martian rock that landed on Earth 13,000 years ago. The jury is still out on whether these are really traces of life that got a foothold when Mars was younger, let alone whether that life still survives today.

This 4.5-billion-year-old Martian rock may contain fossil evidence that primitive life once existed on Mars.

The Martian landscape

Mars is quite a small planet, but everything about it is on a spectacular scale. There's the biggest volcano in the solar system, a huge crack in the crust bigger than Earth's Grand Canyon, crater-scarred plains and the dried-up remains of billion-year-old floods.

MARTIAN VOLCANOES

The most impressive Martian mountain is Mount Olympus, an enormous extinct volcano that towers up to 27 kilometres above the Martian surface. Three times the height of Earth's Mount Everest, Olympus is more than 550 kilometres across. Its sides have shallow slopes, but there are enormous cliffs around its edges, and the volcanic craters at its peak are 85 kilometres wide and surrounded by 3-kilometre-high cliffs.

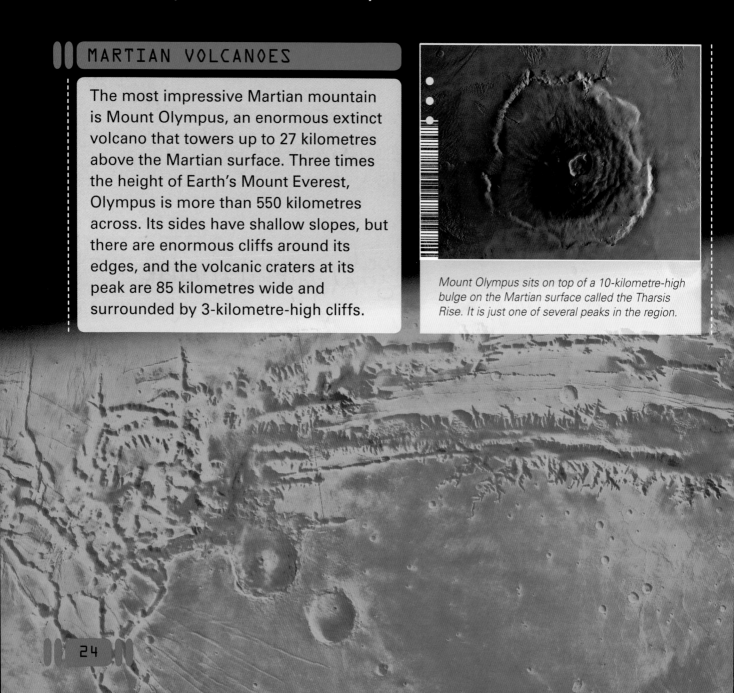

Mount Olympus sits on top of a 10-kilometre-high bulge on the Martian surface called the Tharsis Rise. It is just one of several peaks in the region.

THE GRANDEST CANYON

Longer than North America is wide and up to 7 kilometres deep in places, the Mariner Valleys are a spectacular series of deep, canyon-like gouges in the Martian landscape. They were formed as the planet's crust buckled, distorted and cracked under the weight of the nearby Tharsis Rise. Unlike Earth's Grand Canyon, no river ever ran along this valley, but pools of water may once have collected here. Morning mists and fogs still fill the canyon floor at certain times of the year.

NOT TO MISS

CHRYSE PLANITIA: *A series of huge teardrop-shaped 'islands' in the landscape, formed by a catastrophic flood billions of years ago (see below).*
ALBA PATERA: *A flattened volcanic scar on the Martian surface some 1,600 kilometres long.*
HELLAS: *An enormous impact crater located in the southern highlands of Mars that is now filled with a dusty desert.*
GORGONUM CHAOS: *A series of winding channels through the Martian desert. These channels appear to show evidence that water recently burst to the surface of the planet.*
SYRTIS MAJOR: *A dark spot of exposed volcanic rock that is one of the most obvious features on Mars.*

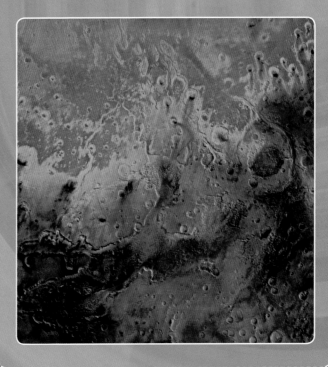

*Named after the **Mariner 9** space probe that first photographed them in 1971, the Mariner Valleys are located along the Martian equator. They extend for nearly a quarter of the planet's circumference.*

Martian weather

Despite its thin atmosphere, Mars has a lot of interesting weather. This ranges from high clouds of carbon dioxide ice crystals to fogs and mists that fill low-lying areas, and from fast-moving dust devils to vast storms that threaten to engulf the entire planet.

STORMY WEATHER

Dust storms are quite common on Mars. Although the air is thin, high winds are widespread, and the Martian dust is so fine that it is easily carried into the air and blown around. Every couple of years, a single storm can cover the entire planet. When such a storm is finally exhausted, the dust can take weeks to settle back to the surface – make sure you pack a dust mask!

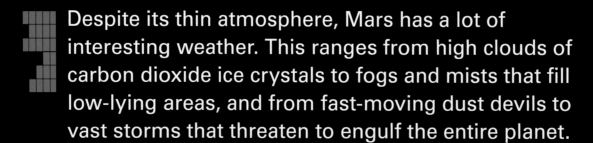

These pictures were taken before and during a Martian dust storm – 26 June 2001 (left) and 4 September 2001 (right).

TRAVELLER'S TIPS - SURVIVING ON MARS

Compared to Mercury, Venus or Earth's Moon, Mars is quite a welcoming holiday prospect, but there are still problems. The air is cold and has no oxygen, so you'll need a spacesuit to protect you. Though the suit needn't be as robust as the type you'd wear on the Moon, the higher gravity on Mars (about one-third of Earth's gravity) will cause problems getting around. Land in the right place and you should be able to extract ice from the soil, which you can melt for drinking water, or process to produce oxygen for breathing and hydrogen for fuel. You'll also need a shelter to protect you from dangerous solar rays and particles that come through the thin atmosphere, and also from those dust storms.

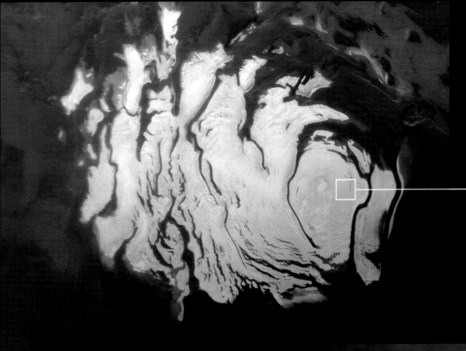

At Mars's south pole (seen here in winter), ice and frozen carbon dioxide are shaped by the planet's powerful winds, creating swirling, cloud-like formations.

POLAR CAPS

Large amounts of frozen water lie buried at Mars's north and south poles – remains of oceans that were much more plentiful when the planet was younger and warmer. These polar icecaps change with the seasons, growing and shrinking as carbon dioxide from the air creates an icy frost that settles over a pole in autumn, and disappears in spring. Over long periods, these patterns of frost have carved the polar icecaps into beautiful swirling patterns.

This view of the north polar cap was taken during the northern Martian summer. The dark area around the cap is made up mainly of sand dunes shaped and formed by wind.

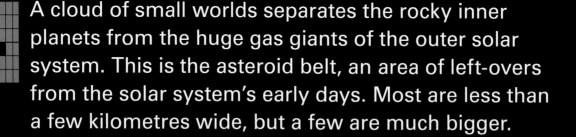

A cloud of small worlds separates the rocky inner planets from the huge gas giants of the outer solar system. This is the asteroid belt, an area of left-overs from the solar system's early days. Most are less than a few kilometres wide, but a few are much bigger.

FORMATION

Astronomers used to think that the asteroids were the shattered remains of a planet. But even if you added up the millions of known asteroids, they still wouldn't be big enough to create a planet. Instead, it seems that the pull of gravity from Mars on one side and Jupiter on the other stopped asteroids in this part of the solar system from clumping together to form anything larger. The largest asteroids are Ceres, with a diameter of 975 kilometres, and 530-kilometre Vesta. Gaspra (see left) is a smaller asteroid, 18 kilometres long.

TRAVELLER'S TIPS - HOW TO AVOID AN ASTEROID

For most of recent history, we've been lucky not to be targeted by an asteroid on a collision course. Astronomers are using high-powered radar to find space rocks with the potential to hit Earth. Meanwhile, scientists are working on ways to divert or deflect anything that gets too close. Blowing up an asteroid with a bomb is a poor solution, since the fragments left behind would carry on along roughly the same orbit and still hit Earth. The shockwave from a bomb in nearby space would deflect a space rock, as would strapping a rocket to one side and pushing it out of the way. Another idea is to use a 'gravity tractor' – a spacecraft flying alongside the asteroid that would pull the rock gently out of the way.

Not all asteroids stay in the asteroid belt. Some have oval orbits that bring them much closer to the Sun on one side – crossing the orbits of Mars or even Earth. Occasionally, these Near-Earth Objects (NEOs) get very close to Earth, or even collide with our planet. Small chunks of rock burn up in Earth's atmosphere, creating trails of light called 'shooting stars'. Anything larger than a few metres across makes it through to hit the surface, sometimes gouging out a spectacular crater.

Meteor Crater in northern Arizona, USA, was created by an asteroid impact 49,000 years ago. The huge crater measures 1,200 metres in diameter and is 170 metres deep.

Glossary

Astronomical body
A physical object, or body, in outer space, such as a comet, moon, planet, star or asteroid (a space rock).

Comet
An astronomical body that travels around the Sun, consisting of a solid, frozen nucleus that vaporises on the approach to the Sun to form glowing tails of gas and dust.

Impact crater
A depression in the surface of a planet, moon or other object, formed by an impact with another astronomical body.

Gravity
The force of attraction that astronomical bodies exert on each other as a result of their mass. The more massive they are, the stronger the gravitational force.

Orbit
The curved path of a physical object in outer space – such as a moon, planet, star or asteroid (a space rock) – around another as a result of strong gravitational attraction.

Planet
An object that follows its own orbit around a star and is massive enough to be shaped by its own gravity into a sphere.

Plate
One of several huge slabs of rock that make up the crust of a planet or moon. Known as tectonic plates, these enormous slabs float on semi-molten rock and interact with neighbouring plates at their boundaries.

Satellite
A physical object in space, such as a moon, orbiting around a planet or star. Man-made satellites include devices placed in orbit around the Earth to relay scientific or communications data.

Solar system
The Sun together with the eight planets – Mercury, Venus, Earth, Mars, Jupiter, Saturn, Uranus and Neptune – and the other astronomical bodies that orbit it.

Volcano
An opening, or rupture, in a planet or moon's crust which allows lava (molten rock heated to extremely high temperatures), ash and gas to escape from below the surface.

World
A term for an astronomical body, typically a planet or moon, but also used to refer to stars, comets and asteroids. Our world, the Earth, is a small, rocky planet with a mass of 5.97 trillion trillion kilograms.

Resources

Universe
General Editor: Martin Rees
(DK, 2005)
An illustrated guide that takes you on a tour from the solar system to the farthest limits of space.

Voyage Across The Cosmos
by Giles Sparrow (Quercus, 2008)
A wealth of facts, information and data about the Universe.

DK Encyclopedia of Space
by Heather Couper and Nigel Henbest
(DK, 2009)
Discover the secrets of the solar system, the galaxy and beyond with this in-depth reference book.

▌▌ QUICK QUIZ

Here are three quick-fire questions to test your knowledge of the inner planets. (Answers at the bottom) Good luck!

1. Which planet will crush, choke and burn you to death if you land there? Is it:
 a) Mercury
 b) Mars
 c) Venus

2. What is Earth's population? Is it:
a) More than 6 billion
b) More than 9 billion
c) More than 12 billion

3. Where did *Apollo 11* land? Is it:
a) Tycho Crater
b) The Sea of Tranquility
c) The Sea of Showers

▌▌ WEBSITES

www.planetary.org/home
A website packed with information about the planets, the exploration of the solar system and the search for extraterrestrial intelligence.

www.universetoday.com
Space exploration and astronomy news brought to you from around the Internet.

www.nasa.gov/audience/forstudents
Scientists from NASA (National Aeronautics and Space Administration) answer your questions on the Universe.

www.space.com
Information on everything to do with space – satellites, stars, astronomy, the Sun, planets, NASA and more.

www.bbc.co.uk/science/space/playspace
Out-of-this-world space puzzles, quizzes and activities to test your knowledge of the solar system's planets and moons.

www.kidsastronomy.com
A comprehensive guide to the Universe, with interactive features and games.

Quiz Answers: 1. c 2. a 3. b

Index

Here are the lists of contents for each title in *Space Travel Guides*